THE BOOK OF CLIMBING KNOTS

For Hugo

THE BOOK OF
CLIMBING KNOTS

PETER OWEN

WARNING

The instructions herein are intended to help you learn how to tie knots in a safe environment. DO NOT use any of these knots in the field without the supervision of a climbing instructor.

The Lyons Press

Design and illustration by Peter Owen

Printed in Canada

10 9 8 7 6 5 4 3 2 1

Library of Congress Cataloging-in-Publication Data

Owen, Peter, 1950–
    The book of climbing knots / Peter Owen.
        p. cm.
    Includes index.
    ISBN 1-55821-988-5 (pb)
    1. Climbing Knots.   I. Title.

GV200.19.K56 O94 2000
796.52'2–dc21   99-089529

CONTENTS

INTRODUCTION

Climbing and mountaineering, like many activities, have undergone some revolutionary changes in recent years. Long gone are the tweed jackets, leather boots, and natural fiber ropes. The highly developed climbing equipment and apparel of today is, in the main, manufactured or constructed from the very latest "high-tech" materials. Apparel is now lightweight, breathable, and totally water- and windproof. Ropes and equipment are now made from artificial or synthetic materials. Arguably the only components, apart from the rocks and mountains, that have changed very little over recent years are the absolutely essential climbing knots.

The Book of Climbing Knots gives you the opportunity to master 30 classic climbing and mountaineering knots. In focusing solely on the knots and not the techniques and skills of climbing, each knot is allocated generous space for clear instructions and meticulous step-by-step illustrations.

The knots are divided into several distinct groups, each of which is used for different purposes. Practice is essential for good knot tying, so select the right knot for the job and practice until you are confident that you can tie it quickly, securely, and literally, with your eyes closed. Your life may depend on it!

ROPES

Rope is the most important piece of equipment that a climber will possess. It must be rope that is specifically designed and manufactured for climbing. Such rope is often referred to as "dynamic"; this means that it will stretch slightly when under load, helping to absorb the shock of a fall, which effectively increases the breaking strain.

Artificial or synthetic materials have almost completely replaced natural fibers in the manufacture of climbing rope. Man-made filaments can be spun to run the whole length of a line, do not vary in thickness, and do not have to be twisted together to make them cohere. This gives them superior strength.

Nylon, first produced in 1938 for domestic use, was the first man-made material to be used in this way. Since then a range of artificial ropes have been developed to meet different purposes, but they all share certain characteristics. Size for size they are lighter, stronger, and cheaper than their natural counterparts. They do not rot or mildew, are resistant to sunlight, chemicals, oil, gasoline, and most common solvents. They can also be made in a range of colors. Color-coded ropes for climbing make for instant recognition of lines of different function and size.

The vast majority of climbing rope in use today is kernmantle rope (see page 10). It is easy to handle, very flexible, and has a good strength-to-weight ratio. Older-style hawser-laid nylon rope (see page 9), is still widely used for training purposes or where cost is a consideration.

Rope manufactured from artificial fiber does have some disadvantages, the main one being that it melts when heated. Even the friction generated when one rope rubs against another may be enough to cause damage, so it is vital to check your ropes regularly. It is also possible for heat friction to fuse knotted rope together so that it is impossible to untie the knot. Another disadvantage is that artificial ropes made of continuous filaments are so smooth that knots slip and come undone. Knots may need to be secured with additional knots.

Choosing a modern climbing rope is no easy task! There is a vast array of designs, sizes, lengths, colors, and prices. The aim of the next few pages is to explain the main differences and how to look after rope. If in doubt about what rope to purchase, always consult an experienced climber or someone at your local climbing equipment store, who in most cases will be very willing to help you.

HAWSER-LAID ROPE

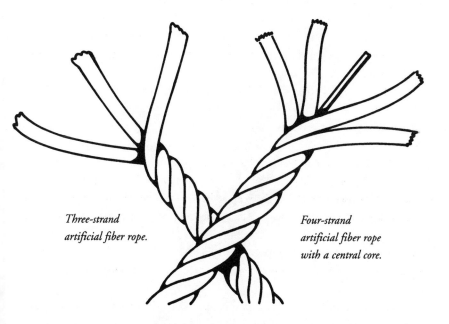

Three-strand artificial fiber rope.

Four-strand artificial fiber rope with a central core.

Artificial rope laid up or twisted like old-style natural fiber rope is known as hawser-laid. Usually three strands of nylon filaments are twisted together to form the rope. There are variations of this available. One very strong variation is four strands of nylon filament twisted around a central nylon core.

The cost of hawser-laid rope is generally about two thirds that of the more widely used kernmantle constructed climbing rope. Laid-up rope, made of thick multifilaments tightly twisted together, may be very resistant to wear, but it may also be difficult to handle because of its stiffness and knots may not hold well. As a general rule, do not buy a rope that is too stiff. Similarly, be wary of twisted rope that is very soft.

This type of rope may be perfectly acceptable for instructional purposes and novice climbing but should be avoided for any serious forms of climbing and should never be used with mechanical rope ascending and belay devices.

KERNMANTLE

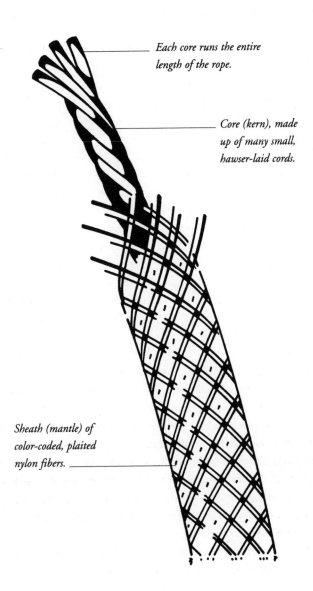

Each core runs the entire length of the rope.

Core (kern), made up of many small, hawser-laid cords.

Sheath (mantle) of color-coded, plaited nylon fibers.

Kernmantle rope is made from synthetic materials having a core, or "kern," of many small, hawser-laid cords contained in a braided sheath, or "mantle." It is this structure that gives the rope all the qualities required for climbing. Kernmantle rope is very strong while being extremely flexible and easy to handle. Its flexibility makes it ideal for knot tying. It has the big climbing advantage of the correct amount of elasticity, helping to absorb the shock of a fall; too much elasticity will increase the the distance fallen by a climber. Good-quality kernmantle climbing rope will give low initial stretch under light loads. The object of this is to minimize wasted effort in rope climbing where, for example, prusiking (see page 96) is involved. This can occur on very big climbs where one person will climb the rock first and the remaining climbers will climb the rope. The smoothness of the outer sheath of kernmantle rope not only makes the rope easy and comfortable to handle but it also allows for good contact and easy use with climbing equipment such as karabiners, descendeurs, and belay devices.

Some climbing ropes are sold featuring various dry treatments. These are highly recommended if climbing in wet or icy conditions. It means that the rope has been chemically treated to repel water. Kernmantle ropes are likely to absorb upwards of 20 percent of their weight in water when used in wet and icy conditions. The disadvantages of this are first, the rope weighs a lot more, counteracting the lightweight qualities of kernmantle; and second, and most crucial, the rope loses strength, possibly as much as 40 percent. Dry treatment will also prevent dirt particles from working their way into the fibers of the rope and causing damage. It is recommended that for all-weather climbing, dry-treated rope, which will generally cost more than untreated rope, is used.

Always buy climbing rope from an approved or recognized dealer. It is now compulsory for all climbing rope to carry descriptive tape tags and labels that clearly state the rope has met all of the standards set by the Union Internationale des Associations d'Alpinisme (UIAA). The UIAA is the governing international body that sets all safety standards adhered to in climbing and mountaineering. With so many variations and types of rope for sale it can be all too easy to confuse, for example, a rope designed for sailing use with a climbing rope. The danger lies in that the sailing rope will not have met any of the stringent tests set by the UIAA. Your approved or recognized dealer will, in most cases, always be willing to help you select and buy the correct climbing rope.

ROPE SIZES AND LENGTHS

Climbing rope is manufactured in a range of sizes, determined by the diameter of the rope, and a range of rope lengths. Different manufactures may produce rope of slightly varying diameters but as a general guide four thicknesses are used in climbing: 5mm (¹/₄ in), 7mm (¹/₃ in), 9mm (³/₈ in), and 11mm (¹/₂ in). The equivalent thicknesses in hawser-laid rope are 1, 2, 3, and 4.

Standard rope lengths are 45m (150ft), 50m (165ft), and 60m (195ft). Check with your approved or recognized dealer for any different rope sizes. They will, in most cases, be keen to offer advice without prejudice on all climbing equipment.

All synthetic rope ends can be sealed using heat. When you buy standard lengths of rope the ends will be factory sealed. If you should need to cut synthetic rope yourself, use a sharp knife and then melt the end with a cigarette lighter or on an electric ring.

5mm (¹/₄ in) rope
These light, flexible ropes are used for threading through climbing protection devices and for creating prusik loops.

7mm (¹/₃ in) rope
These ropes are used for threading through medium-size climbing protection devices.

9mm (³⁄₈ in) double or half rope

Many climbing techniques use a pair of ropes. This rope is specifically designed to be used in pairs and is best suited for mountaineering, alpine climbing, and long rock climbs.

9mm (³⁄₈ in) single rope

This lightweight rope is designed to be used singly and is favored by sport climbers where weight is a priority. It is also used for threading through large climbing protection devices.

11mm (¹⁄₂ in) rope

This rope is the main climbing rope, used for general rock climbing. It is an all-around rope and works well on everything from sports to long free routes. It has a good strength-to-weight ratio and it can also be used for slings.

LOOKING AFTER ROPE

Climbing rope is sturdy material, but it is expensive, so it's worth looking after it properly. Caring for rope and using it correctly will help it keep its strength and prolong its life. Here are some guidelines for good rope care.

- Avoid dragging rope over rough, sharp edges, or dirty, gritty surfaces where particles could get into the rope and damage it.

- Do not walk on rope.

- Do not force rope into harsh kinks.

- Do not use as a tow rope or for anything else other than climbing purposes.

- Inspect rope regularly and wash off any dirt or grit with a mild detergent.

- If rope has been in salt water, rinse thoroughly to remove all salt deposits.

- Always store rope in a dry place, out of sunlight, and away from such things as car battery acid.

- If rope has been damaged in any way or has sustained a severe fall it should be discarded in the interests of safety.

- If knots are repeatedly tied in one section of rope, that section will weaken.

- Always use your own ropes for climbing, preferably ones that you have bought. If you borrow a rope, make sure you know its history.

- The life of a climbing rope obviously depends on the amout of use, but as a general rule rope should be dicarded and replaced after two to three years.

- Finally, never use two ropes of different material together, because only the more rigid of the two will work under strain.

ROPE DAMAGE

Core damage can be detected by lumps or bulges in the rope. The sheath can be unaffected by this and show no external damage. As the main strength of the rope is in the core, this is extremely dangerous and the rope should be discarded immediately.

Sheath damage is usually the result of the rope rubbing across a sharp edge, or a sharp stone or rock dropping onto the rope. The core will often be unaffected by this damage but the rope is now unsafe and should be discarded immediately.

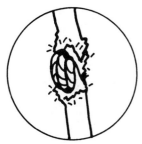

COILING ROPE

Coiling a rope will ensure that it will be immediately at hand and untangled when required.

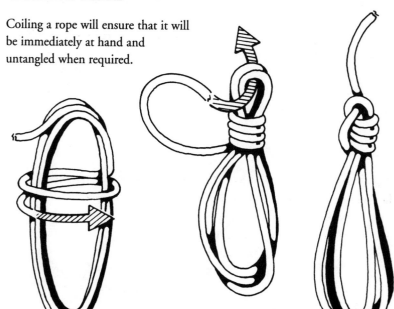

HOW TO USE THIS BOOK

The diagrams accompanying the descriptions of the knots are intended to be self-explanatory, but for added clarity, sequenced, written instructions and special tying techniques and methods do accompany the knots. There are arrows to show the directions in which you should push or pull the working ends and standing parts of the rope or line. The dotted lines indicate intermediate positions of the rope. When tying the knot you should always have a sufficient working end to complete the knot. The amount of working end required can often be calculated by looking at the illustration of the finished knot. Always follow the order shown of going over or under a length of line; reversing or changing this order could result in a completely different knot, which might well be unstable, unsafe, and insecure.

ROPE PARTS

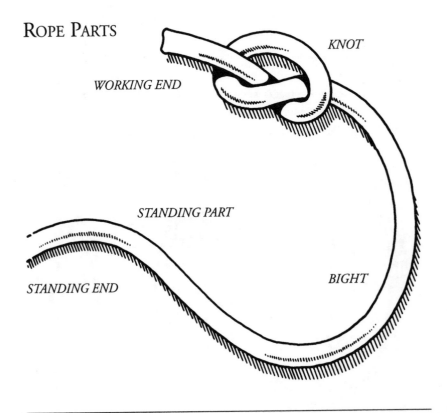

KNOT

WORKING END

STANDING PART

STANDING END

BIGHT

WARNING

Friction-generated heat may cause synthetic rope to weaken and break without warning (see page 8). Rock climbers and mountaineers should exercise extreme caution when using synthetic rope in situations that may cause friction damage. **The result could be fatal.**

STOPPER KNOTS

Stopper knots, as their name suggests, are used to prevent the end of a rope or line from slipping through an eye, loop, or hole. They can be used to bind the end of a rope so that it will not unravel, weight the end of a rope for throwing purposes, and for decoration.

Many climbing knots, for example, the climber's bowline (see page 62) can be finished off with a stopper knot tied in the working end for extra security.

FIGURE-EIGHT KNOT

This is a quick and efficient way of tying a simple and attractive stopper knot at the end of a line or rope. The knot's name comes from its characteristic shape. Its interlaced appearance has long been seen as a symbol of interwoven affection. In heraldry it signifies faithful love and appears on various coats of arms—hence its other names, the Flemish or Savoy knot.

1. Double over the rope and twist the end to form a loop.

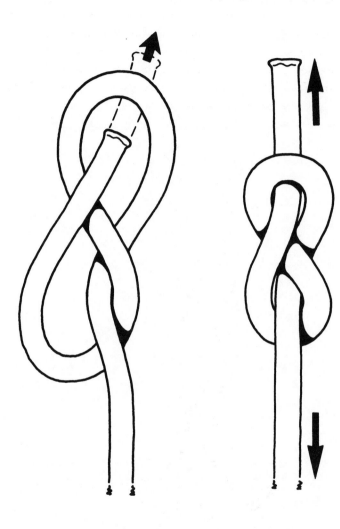

2. *Pass the working end over the standing part and then up through the loop.*

3. *Pull on both the working end and the standing part to form the knot.*

HEAVING LINE KNOT

This stopper knot has the advantage of adding considerable weight to the end of the line. This proves particularly useful for throwing the end of a line across a gap or to another climber.

The heaving line knot is widely used by sailors, who tie it at the end of a lighter line, which in turn is attached to a heavier line. The lighter line is thrown first, usually from boat to shore, so the heavier line can then be drawn or heaved behind it.

The knot's other name, the monk's knot, derives from its use by Franciscan monks to weight the ends of the cords they use as belts.

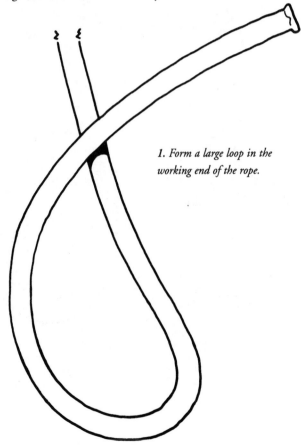

1. Form a large loop in the working end of the rope.

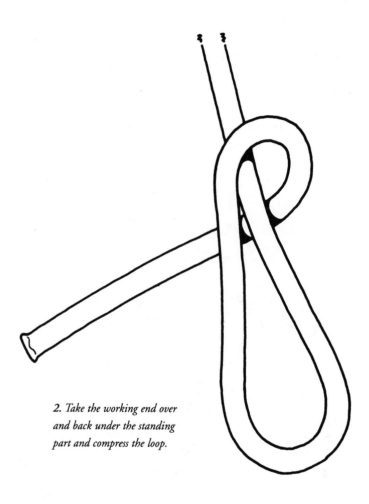

2. Take the working end over and back under the standing part and compress the loop.

continued on page 24

Heaving Line Knot

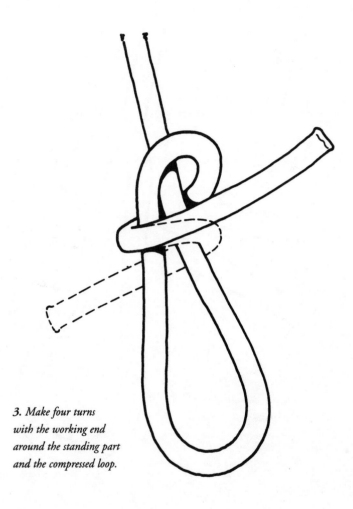

3. Make four turns
with the working end
around the standing part
and the compressed loop.

4. *On the fourth turn take the working end down through the loop. Keep the already formed turns as tight as possible.*

5. *Pull on the working end and the standing part to tighten the knot. As the knot is tightening, form the final knot shape.*

BENDS

B ends are used to join two lengths of rope at their ends to form one longer piece. It is important, if bends are to be secure, for the ropes joined in this way to be of the same kind and the same diameter.

The sheet bend (see "Essential Outdoor Knots," page 118) is the exception to this rule. It is very secure, even when it is used to join ropes of different diameters.

FISHERMAN'S KNOT

It is known that this classic knot was used by the ancient Greeks. It is generally known as the fisherman's knot, but over the years it has picked up many different names (including English knot, halibut knot, and waterman's knot).

It is formed from two overhand knots (see page 114) that jam against each other. After use, the two component knots are generally easily separated and undone. The fisherman's knot should be used to join lines of equal thickness and is not suitable for large-diameter rope.

NOTE: The fisherman's knot and the fisherman's bend (see page 134) are quite different and should not be confused with each other.

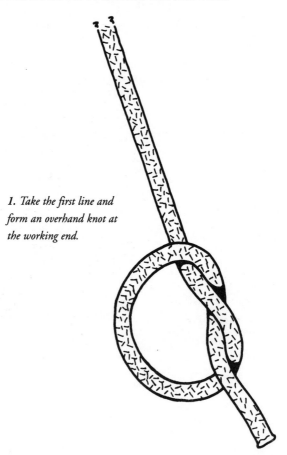

1. Take the first line and form an overhand knot at the working end.

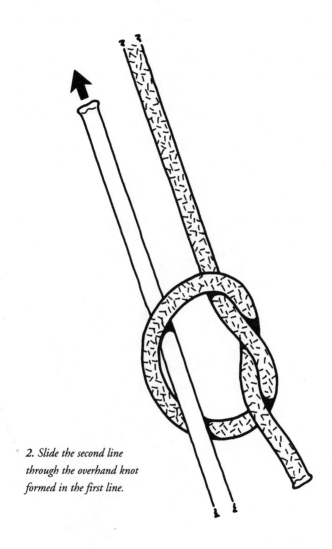

2. Slide the second line through the overhand knot formed in the first line.

continued on page 30

Fisherman's Knot

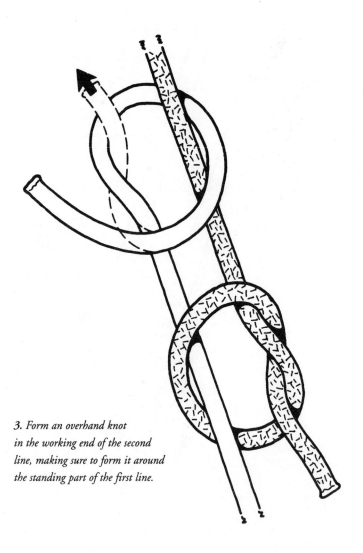

3. Form an overhand knot
in the working end of the second
line, making sure to form it around
the standing part of the first line.

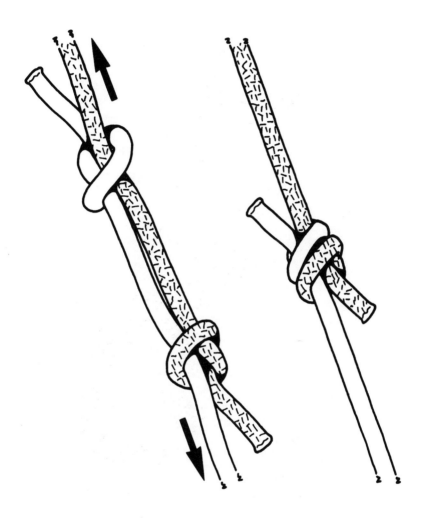

4. *Tighten both of the overhand knots and slowly draw them together by pulling on the standing part of each line.*

5. *Continue pulling on the standing parts until the two overhand knots are jammed firmly together. The knot is now complete.*

DOUBLE FISHERMAN'S KNOT

This extension of the fisherman's knot is one of the most widely used climbing knots and is one of the safest ways to join rope or cord. It is probably the best way to create a sling (loop) from a single piece of rope or cord.

It is good practice to seize the ends of the knot with sticky tape to keep them from catching on the rock face and to minimize the risk of the knot's working loose.

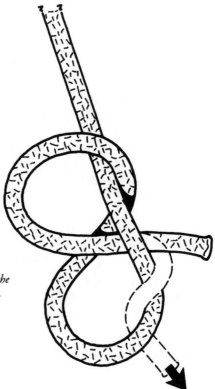

1. Form a double overhand knot in the working end of the first line.

2. Slide the second line through both sections of the double overhand knot formed in the first line.

continued on page 34

Double Fisherman's Knot

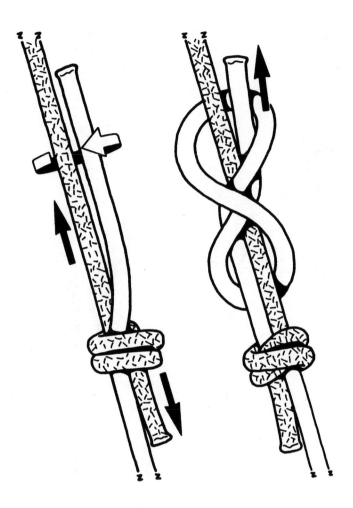

3. Tighten the double overhand knot in the first line. It helps at this point to turn the knot assembly over.

4. Form a double overhand knot in the working end of the second line, making sure to form it around the standing part of the first line.

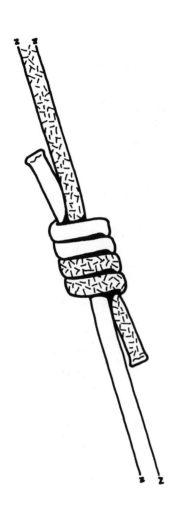

5. *Tighten the second double overhand knot and pull on both standing parts until the two knots are jammed firmly together. The knot is now complete.*

6. *Seize the ends of the knot with sticky tape to keep them from catching on the rock face and to minimize the risk of the knot's working loose.*

CARRICK BEND

This knot is formed from two overhand knots crossing each other. It is a very stable knot, does not slip, and is a very secure way of joining two ropes of similar diameter but different type. It can be used to tie heavy ropes together, but this does form a bulky knot that is unsuitable, for example, for passing through a karabiner.

In its flat form before it is fully drawn together it is valued for its distinctive symmetric appearance and can often be seen in various forms of design.

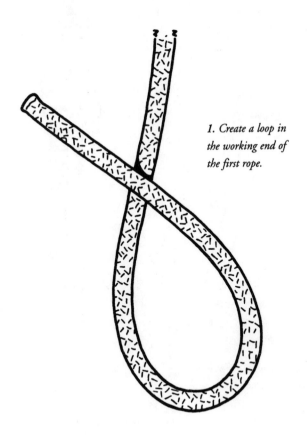

1. Create a loop in the working end of the first rope.

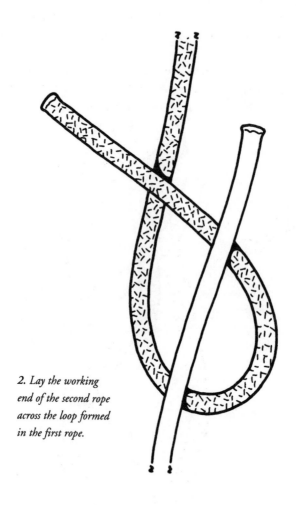

2. Lay the working end of the second rope across the loop formed in the first rope.

continued on page 38

Carrick Bend

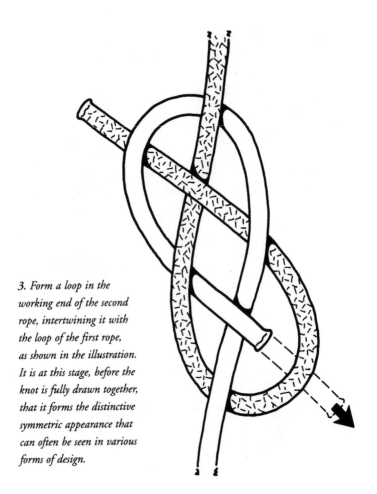

3. *Form a loop in the working end of the second rope, intertwining it with the loop of the first rope, as shown in the illustration. It is at this stage, before the knot is fully drawn together, that it forms the distinctive symmetric appearance that can often be seen in various forms of design.*

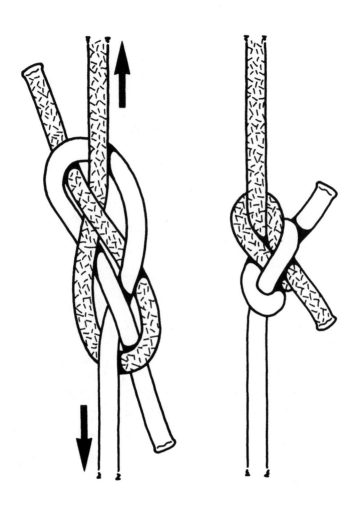

4. *Slowly draw the knot together by pulling on both standing parts.*

5. *Continue to draw the knot tight until the two loops lock together.*

HUNTER'S BEND

The Hunter's, or rigger's, bend is based on two overhand knots. It is strong, stable, and has a good grip and the advantage of being easy to untie.

It is named after Dr. Edward Hunter, a retired physician, who was reported to have invented it in 1968. Subsequent research, however, revealed that the same knot had been described nearly twenty years earlier by Phil D. Smith, in an American publication called *Knots for Mountaineers*. He had devised the knot while working on the waterfront in San Francisco and called it the rigger's bend. Whoever first invented it, the Hunter's, or rigger's, bend remains a good knot with many useful qualities.

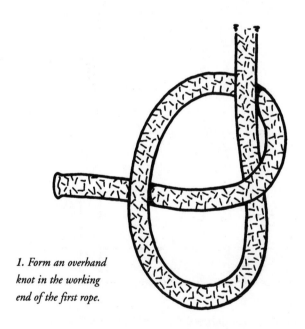

1. Form an overhand knot in the working end of the first rope.

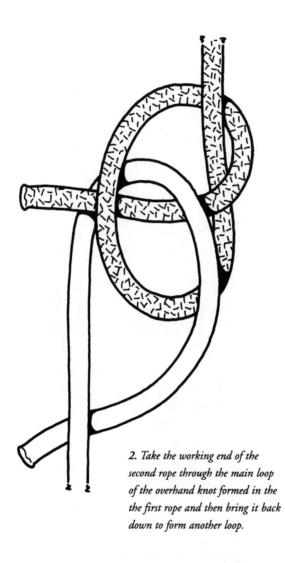

2. *Take the working end of the second rope through the main loop of the overhand knot formed in the the first rope and then bring it back down to form another loop.*

continued on page 42

Hunter's Bend

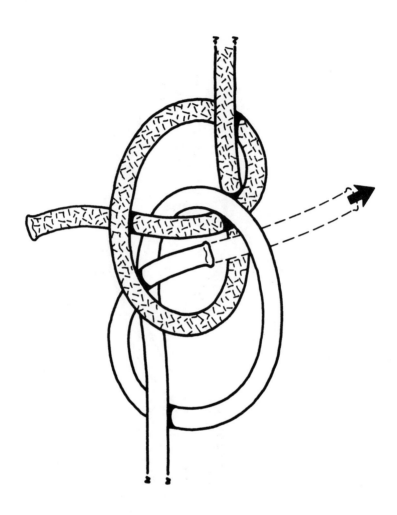

3. Form an overhand knot in the working end of
the second rope, intertwining it with the overhand
knot of the first rope, as shown in the illustration.

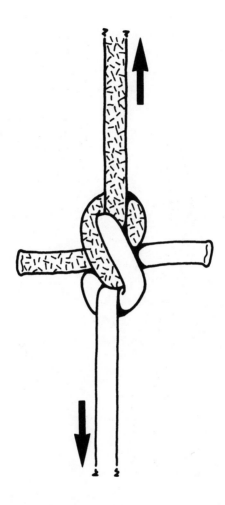

4. Tighten the knot by pulling on both standing parts until the two overhand knots lock together. The knot is now complete.

TAPE KNOT

Most "tapes" are sewn into slings at the manufacturing stage. Should you ever need to tie two tape ends together, use the tape knot.

It is a relatively simple knot to tie and after you have drawn the knot tight it is advisable to seize the ends with sticky tape to minimize the possibility of the knot's working loose. As with all climbing knots, you should check the knot regularly to ensure it is still tied firmly.

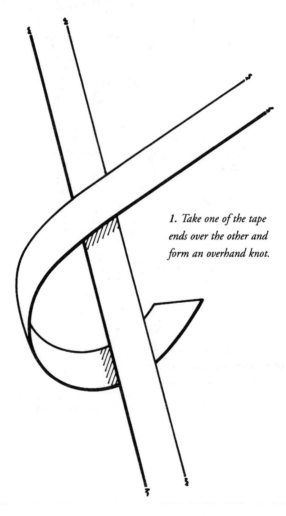

1. Take one of the tape ends over the other and form an overhand knot.

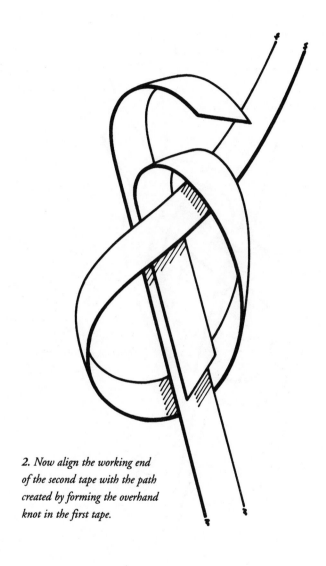

2. Now align the working end of the second tape with the path created by forming the overhand knot in the first tape.

continued on page 46

Tape Knot

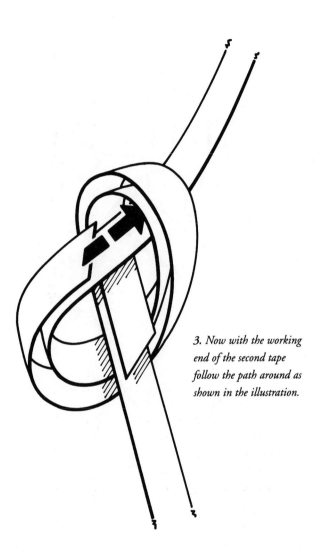

3. Now with the working end of the second tape follow the path around as shown in the illustration.

4. Tighten the knot by pulling on both the standing parts until the two overhand knots mesh together. Seize the tape ends with sticky tape to keep them from catching on the rock face and to minimize the risk of the knot's working loose.

LOOPS

Knots made in the end of a rope by folding it back into an eye or loop and then knotting it to its own standing part are called loops. They are fixed and do not slide.

Loops are particularly important to climbers who find these knots indispensable for tying on and when using anchors.

Figure-Eight Loop

This is one of the best known and most widely used of all climbing knots. It is probably the safest way to form a loop in the main climbing rope and is regularly used for tying on and attaching to anchors.

It is comparatively easy to tie and stays tied. Its disadvantages—it is difficult to adjust and cannot easily be untied after loading—tend to be outweighed by its general usefulness.

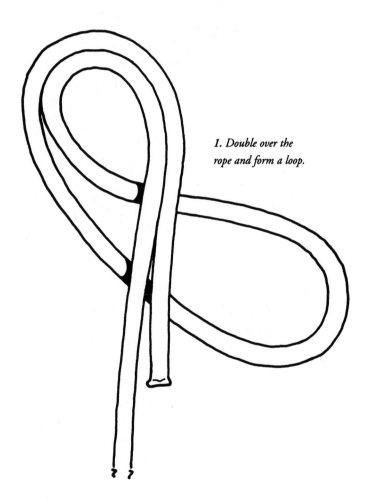

1. Double over the rope and form a loop.

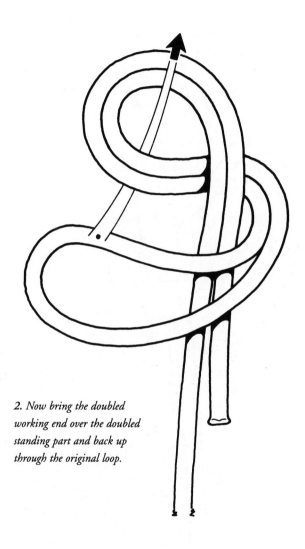

2. Now bring the doubled working end over the doubled standing part and back up through the original loop.

continued on page 52

Figure-Eight Loop

3. Pull the doubled working end through the original loop and slowly draw the knot together by pulling the loop and the main standing part.

4. *Tighten the final knot, making sure that the figure-eight pattern and the loop have been correctly formed.*

THREADED FIGURE-EIGHT

This variation of the figure-eight loop is used when you want to tie a loop around something rather than drop it over or onto something. This knot is most widely used for "tying on"—securely connecting a rope to a harness. For added security, a stopper knot should be added.

Tying on using a correctly tied threaded figure-eight knot is a maneuver that all climbers should be able to do with their eyes closed!

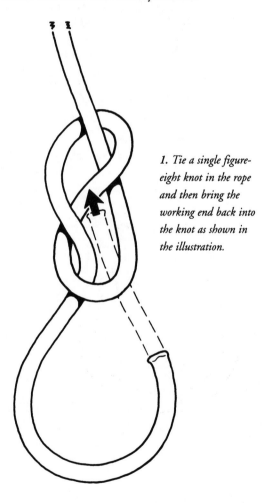

1. Tie a single figure-eight knot in the rope and then bring the working end back into the knot as shown in the illustration.

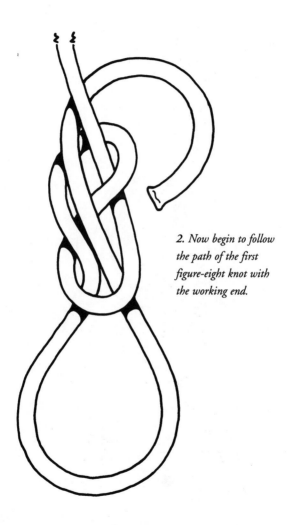

2. *Now begin to follow
the path of the first
figure-eight knot with
the working end.*

continued on page 56

Threaded Figure-Eight

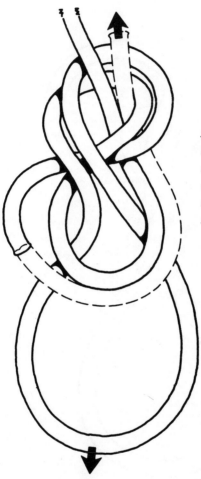

3. Continue to follow
the path of the original
knot and bring the
working end out
in line with the
standing part.

4. *Tighten and form the final knot. A stopper knot can be added at this stage for extra security.*

ALPINE BUTTERFLY KNOT

This knot is used to create a secure loop in a line or rope. It can be a difficult knot to tie, so practice is required. But on the plus side, it unties easily, does not slip, and the loop does not shrink when the knot is tightened.

Once a very popular climbing knot, the alpine butterfly knot has now lost some of its popularity due to other emerging climbing knots and newly designed equipment, but it still remains a very secure and effective loop.

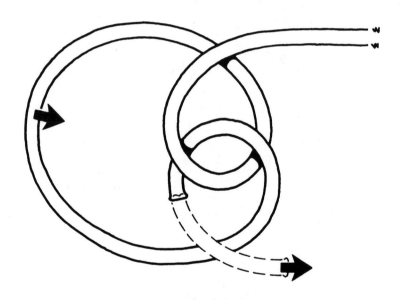

1. Form a loop in the rope, bring the working end around through the loop, and form another loop.

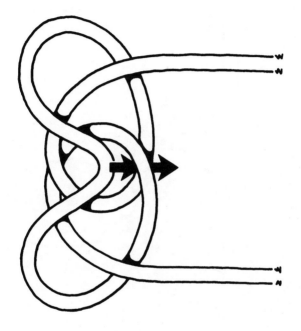

2. *Create the rope pattern shown in the illustration and push the bight of the rope through in the direction of the arrows.*

continued on page 60

Alpine Butterfly Knot

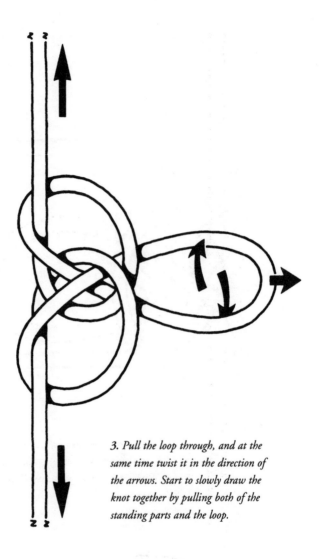

3. *Pull the loop through, and at the same time twist it in the direction of the arrows. Start to slowly draw the knot together by pulling both of the standing parts and the loop.*

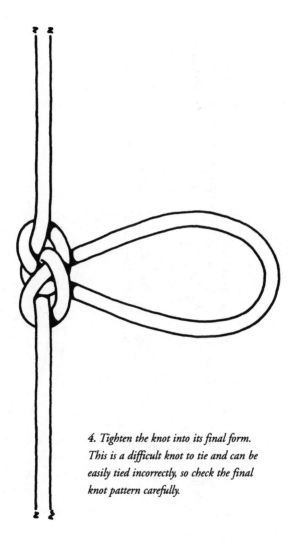

*4. Tighten the knot into its final form.
This is a difficult knot to tie and can be
easily tied incorrectly, so check the final
knot pattern carefully.*

CLIMBER'S BOWLINE

A climber's bowline is also known as a bulin knot. It is a classic knot for tying on and has the advantage of being easy to adjust. It can be used either when tying on around the waist or to a harness.

A note of caution: Although the climber's bowline is fast to tie and easily untied, it does have a tendency to work loose, especially if the rope is new or stiff. It should always, therefore, be used in conjunction with a stopper knot.

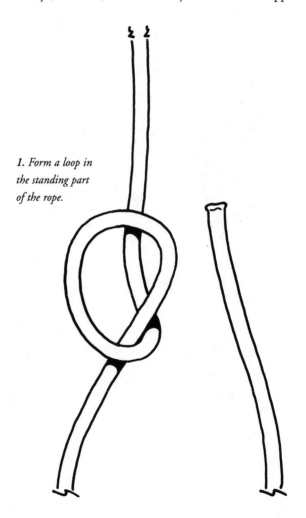

1. Form a loop in the standing part of the rope.

2. Pull the standing part of the rope through the loop to form a secondary loop.

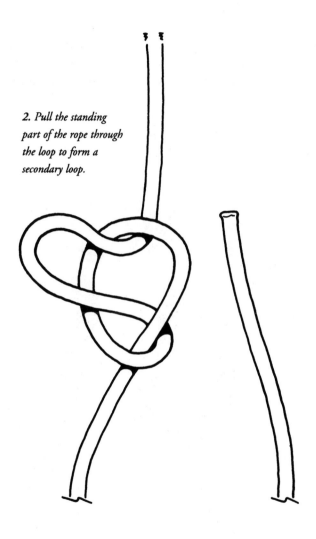

continued on page 64

Climber's Bowline

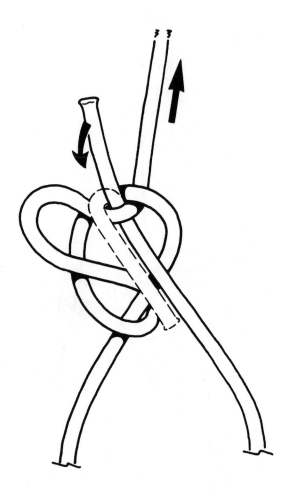

3. Push the working end through the secondary loop and pull it straight back over as shown in the illustration. Pull the standing part and the knot will form.

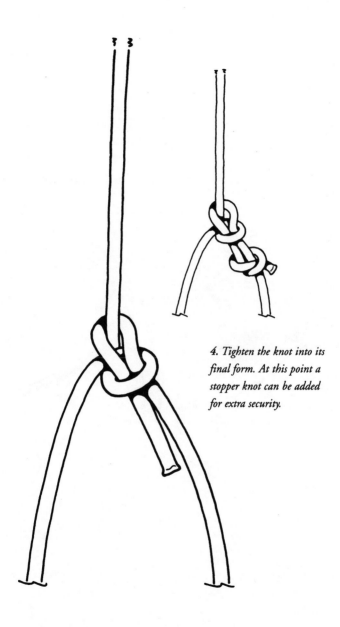

4. Tighten the knot into its final form. At this point a stopper knot can be added for extra security.

SPANISH BOWLINE

This is a very strong knot that has been widely used in mountain rescue work and is also known as the chair knot. It is formed by two separate and independent loops that will hold securely and are very safe, even under considerable strain.

To effect a rescue, one loop is slipped over the casualty's head, around the back, and under the armpits; the other loop goes around the legs behind the knees. It is vitally important that each loop is tightened to the individual's size and locked into position, otherwise an unconscious casualty could easily fall through the loops.

The Spanish bowline is also a very useful for hoisting large objects and pieces of equipment.

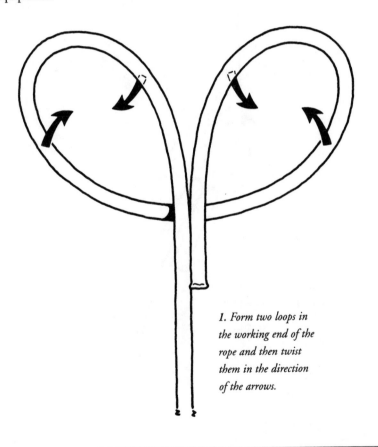

1. Form two loops in the working end of the rope and then twist them in the direction of the arrows.

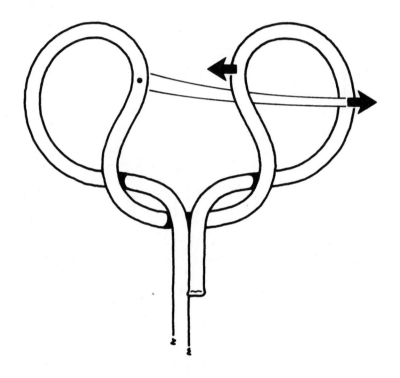

*2. Pull the left-hand twisted loop
through the right-hand twisted loop.*

continued on page 68

Spanish Bowline

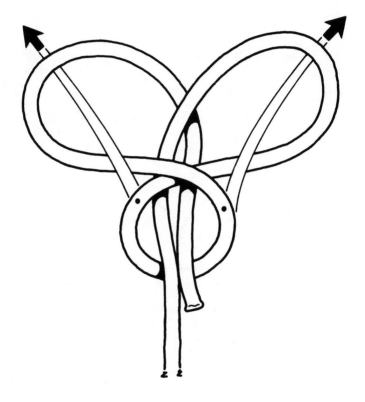

3. Pull the two indicated points of
the newly formed lower loop through
the upper loops.

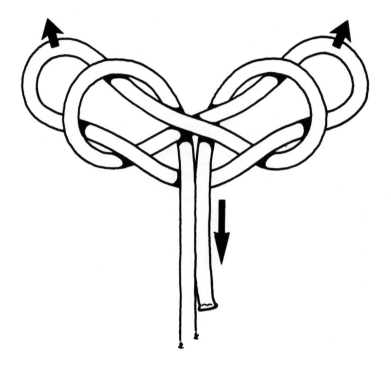

4. Slowly pull on the three points
indicated by the arrows, making sure
that the knot keeps its pattern and shape.

continued on page 70

Spanish Bowline

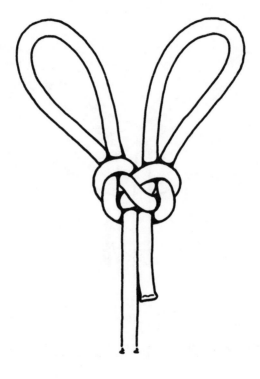

5. *Before tightening the knot into its final form, adjust the loops to the required sizes.*

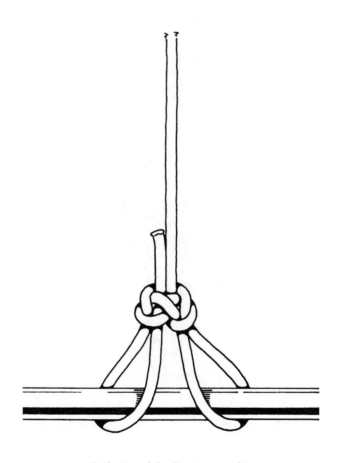

6. *The Spanish bowline is very useful for hoisting large objects and pieces of equipment.*

SHORTENINGS

Shortenings are invaluable knots, well worth mastering. As their name suggests, they are used to shorten lengths of rope or line without cutting. A rope shortened by means of a knot can always be lengthened later, and a single unbroken line will always be more secure than two lines knotted together.

Shortenings can be used as an emergency measure to take up damaged lengths of climbing rope. The weakened sections are incorporated into the knot and are not, therefore, subject to strain.

SHEEPSHANK

The sheepshank can be used to shorten any rope to any required length without cutting. It is easy to tie, holds under tension with a good jamming action, does not change its shape, and unties easily.

In a climbing emergency a sheepshank can be used to shorten a damaged line or rope, but take care to ensure that the damaged or weakened section of the rope passes through both half hitches.

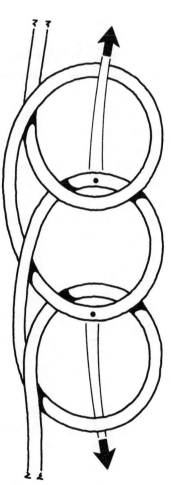

1. Form three loops at the point in the rope where the shortening will be required. Pull the indicated points of the middle loop through the two outer loops.

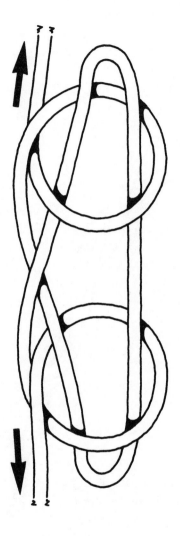

*2. Slowly pull on the two main parts
of the rope, making sure that the knot
retains it, shape and form.*

continued on page 76

Sheepshank

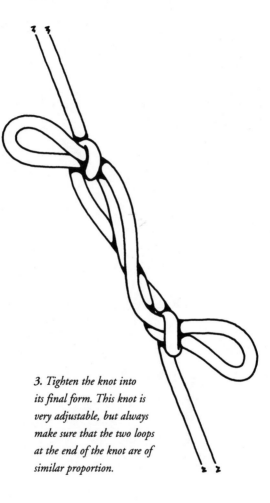

3. Tighten the knot into
its final form. This knot is
very adjustable, but always
make sure that the two loops
at the end of the knot are of
similar proportion.

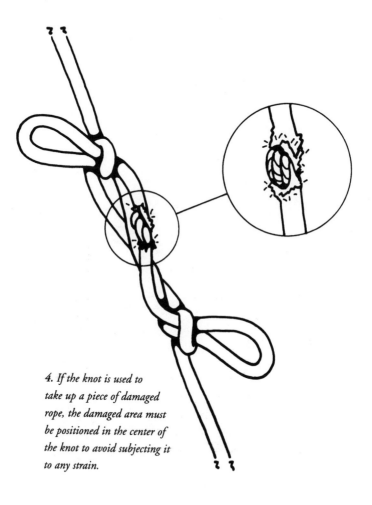

4. *If the knot is used to take up a piece of damaged rope, the damaged area must be positioned in the center of the knot to avoid subjecting it to any strain.*

LOOP KNOT

This knot can be used to form a quick and simple loop in a rope or, more important, it can be used in an emergency to shorten a damaged rope. The weakened or damaged section of the rope is taken up in the center of the knot, where it cannot be put under any strain.

Should your climbing ropes become weakened or damage, dispose of them at the first opportunity. The risks involved in using damaged or weakened rope for any climbing activities are too great!

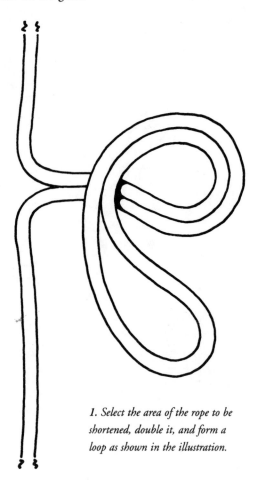

1. Select the area of the rope to be shortened, double it, and form a loop as shown in the illustration.

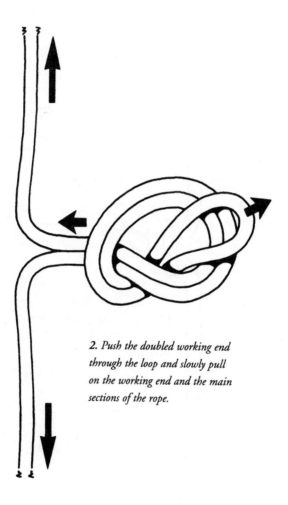

2. Push the doubled working end through the loop and slowly pull on the working end and the main sections of the rope.

continued on page 80

Loop Knot

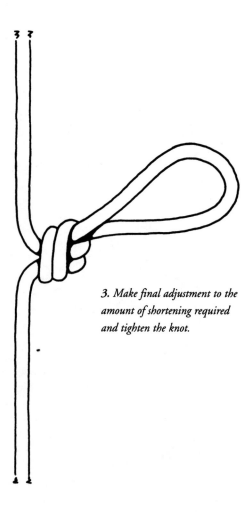

3. Make final adjustment to the amount of shortening required and tighten the knot.

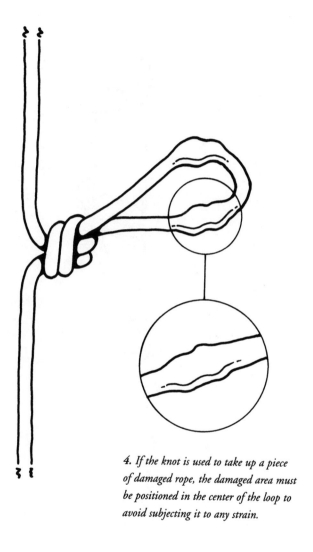

4. If the knot is used to take up a piece of damaged rope, the damaged area must be positioned in the center of the loop to avoid subjecting it to any strain.

HITCHES

Hitches are knots used to secure a rope to another object (such as a karabiner, protection device, stake), or to another rope that does not play any part in the actual tying, for example, attaching a sling to the main climbing rope.

CLOVE HITCH

The clove hitch is one of the best known and most valuable of general hitches. Its main climbing use is to attach line or rope to metal pegs or stakes. It is a relatively easy knot to tie and can, with practice, be tied with just one hand, which is essential because its normal use is in situations where speed is essential.

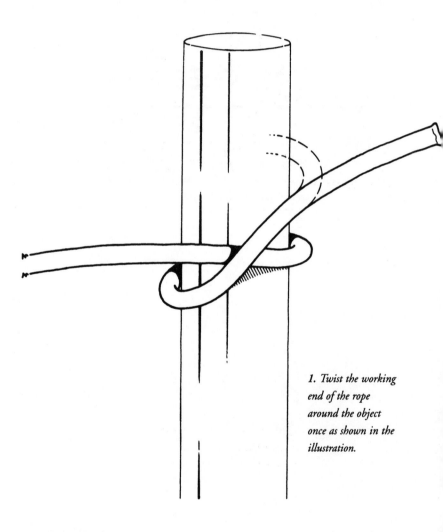

1. Twist the working end of the rope around the object once as shown in the illustration.

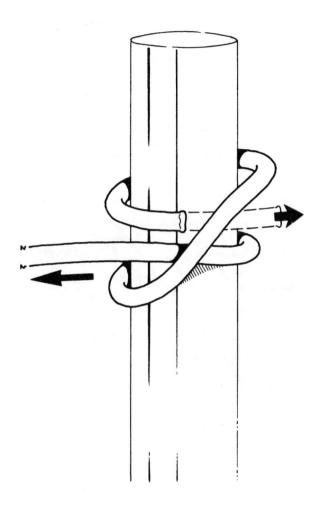

2. Twist the working end a second time, directing it out underneath the crossed-over section of the first twist.

continued on page 86

Clove Hitch

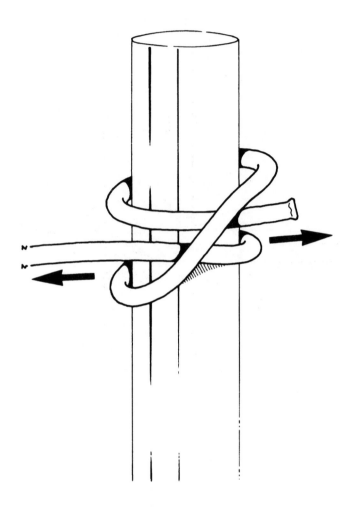

3. Slowly pull the working end and the standing part, making sure that the knot keeps its pattern and shape.

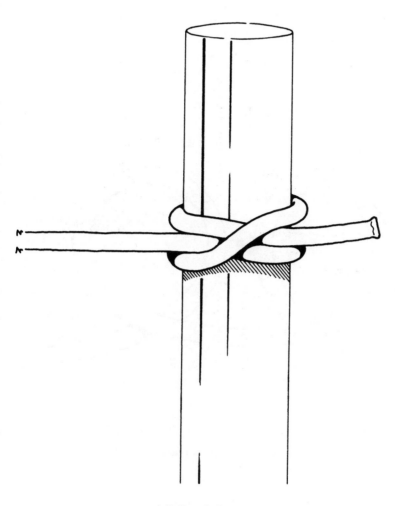

4. Tighten the knot into its final form.

CLOVE HITCH—OVER A STAKE

This variation of the clove hitch is dropped over a peg or stake rather than tied around the object. It is formed by two overlapping half hitches and with practice can be tied very quickly. It is specifically used to attach a tape sling to a peg or stake.

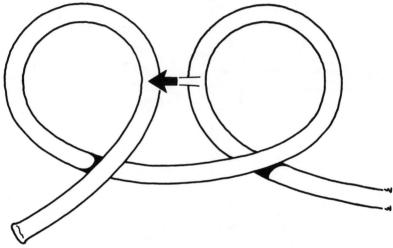

1. Form two loops in the working end of the rope and pull the right-hand loop over the top of the left-hand loop.

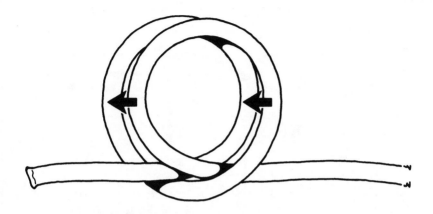

2. Position the two loops on top of each other.

3. Adjust the size of the loops to fit the object.

continued on page 90

Clove Hitch—Over a Stake

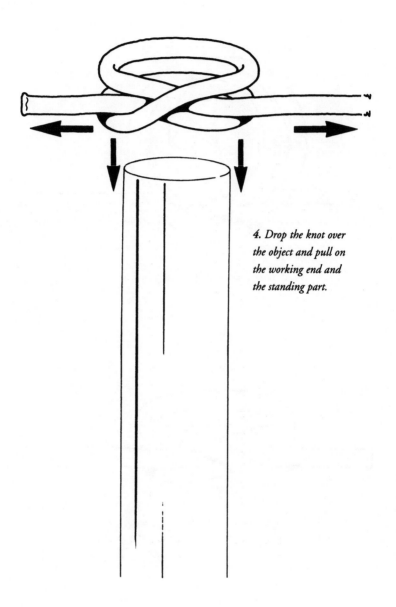

4. Drop the knot over
the object and pull on
the working end and
the standing part.

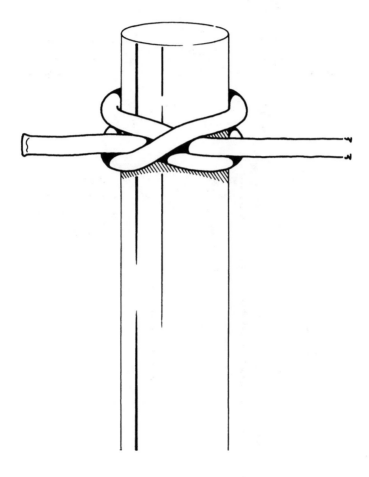

5. Tighten the knot into its final form.

CLOVE HITCH—MADE ON A RING

This further variation of the clove hitch is specifically used to attach a line or rope to a ring or similar construction. It is possible to quickly loosen and re-tighten this knot to control or regulate the length of line leading to the ring or similar construction.

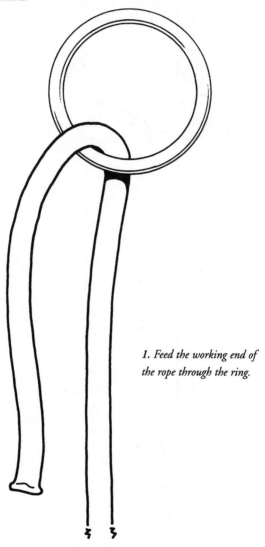

1. Feed the working end of the rope through the ring.

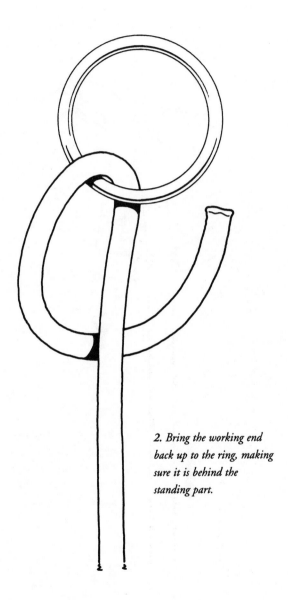

2. Bring the working end back up to the ring, making sure it is behind the standing part.

continued on page 94

Clove Hitch—Made on a Ring

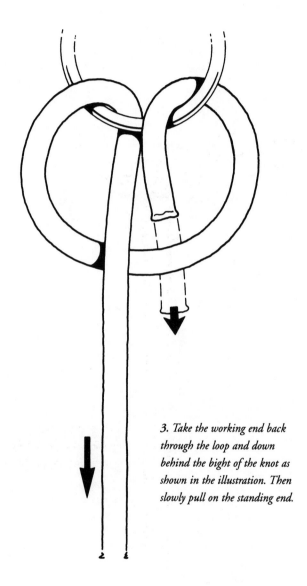

3. Take the working end back through the loop and down behind the bight of the knot as shown in the illustration. Then slowly pull on the standing end.

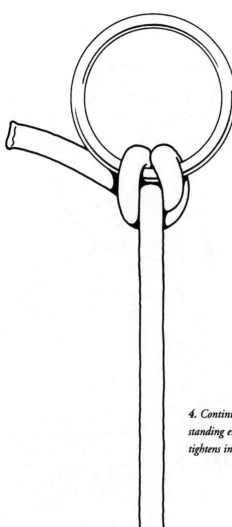

4. Continue to pull on the standing end until the knot tightens into its final form.

PRUSIK KNOT

This knot was devised by Dr. Carl Prusik in 1931. It is used to attach slings to the main climbing rope in such a way that they slide freely when the knot is loose but hold firm under a sideways load.

The Prusik knot does not always slide easily and, once the load is in place, it can only be released by removing the weight and freeing the turns of the rope. The knot must be tied with rope that is considerably thinner than the main climbing rope, and it is important to remember that the knot can slip if the rope is wet or icy.

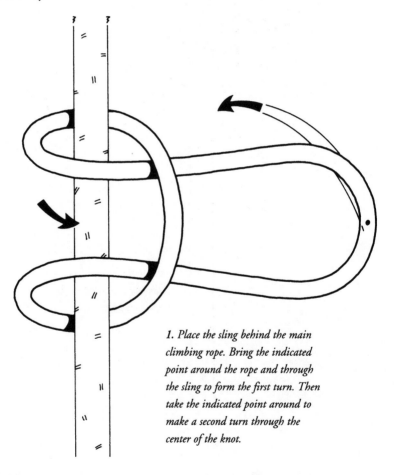

1. Place the sling behind the main climbing rope. Bring the indicated point around the rope and through the sling to form the first turn. Then take the indicated point around to make a second turn through the center of the knot.

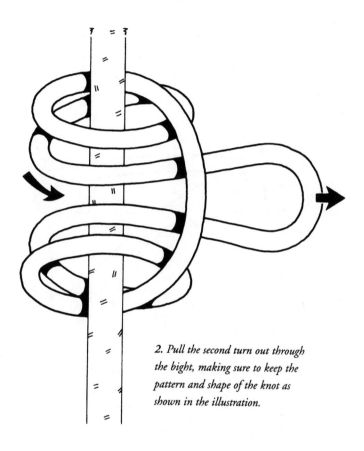

2. Pull the second turn out through the bight, making sure to keep the pattern and shape of the knot as shown in the illustration.

continued on page 98

Prusik Knot

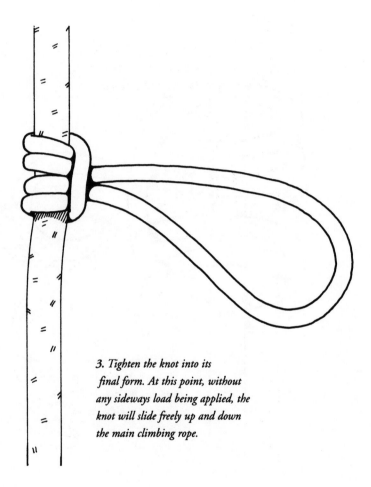

3. *Tighten the knot into its
final form. At this point, without
any sideways load being applied, the
knot will slide freely up and down
the main climbing rope.*

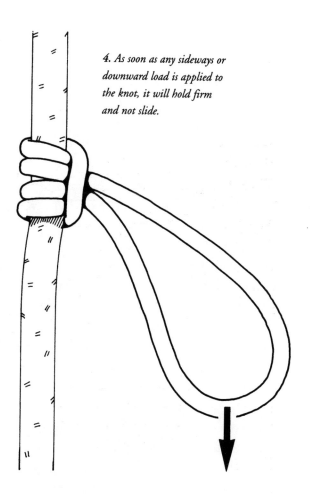

4. As soon as any sideways or downward load is applied to the knot, it will hold firm and not slide.

BACHMANN HITCH

This knot is a very useful alternative to the Prusik knot. It moves more easily, is less likely to jam, and works better on wet and icy ropes. It is tied in combination with a screwgate karabiner, which in turn provides a good handhold.

It is essential that the Bachmann knot is tied with rope much thinner than the main climbing rope. Practice tying this knot with one hand.

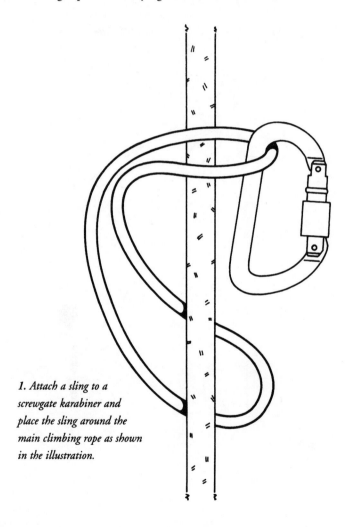

1. Attach a sling to a screwgate karabiner and place the sling around the main climbing rope as shown in the illustration.

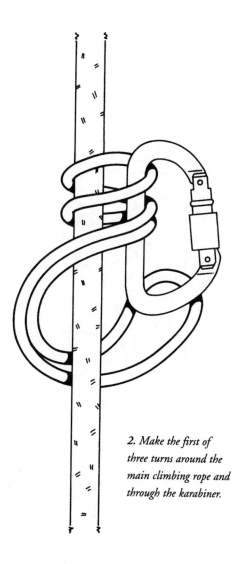

2. Make the first of three turns around the main climbing rope and through the karabiner.

continued on page 102

Bachmann Hitch

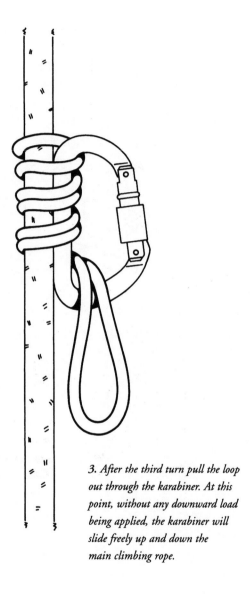

3. After the third turn pull the loop out through the karabiner. At this point, without any downward load being applied, the karabiner will slide freely up and down the main climbing rope.

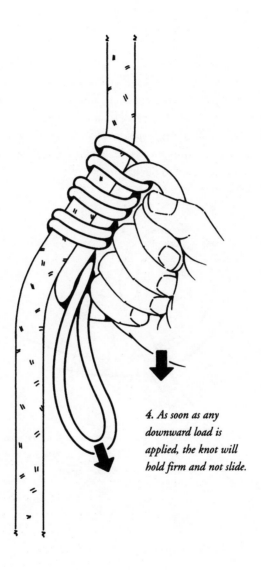

4. As soon as any downward load is applied, the knot will hold firm and not slide.

ITALIAN HITCH

The Italian hitch is an innovative climbing knot used for belaying, and was introduced into the mountaineers' lexicon of knots in 1974. Its chief advantage lies in its means of absorbing the energy of a fall.

The climbing rope is attached to a karabiner with an Italian hitch and this will check a climber's fall by locking up. The knot also allows the climbing rope to be paid out or pulled in to provide slack or tension when required.

It is the official means of belaying (that is, fixing a running rope around a rock or cleat) of the Union Internationale des Associations d'Alpinisme. The major disadvantage of this knot, also called the munter friction hitch or sliding ring hitch, is that it is easy to tie incorrectly.

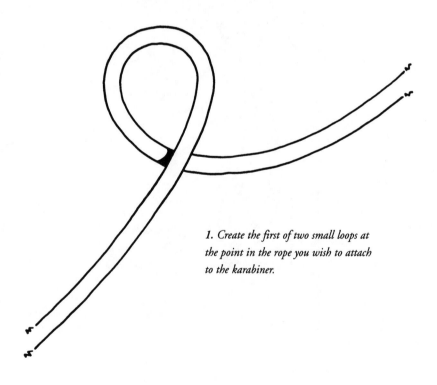

1. Create the first of two small loops at the point in the rope you wish to attach to the karabiner.

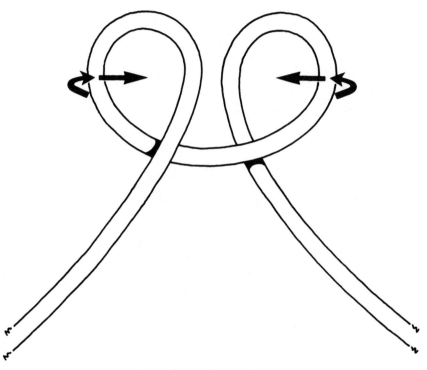

2. Create the second loop in the opposite way to the first, as shown above. Pull the two loops together in the direction of the arrows.

continued on page 106

Italian Hitch

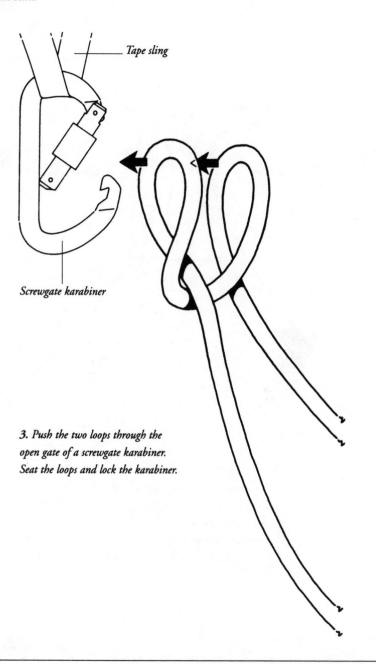

Tape sling

Screwgate karabiner

3. Push the two loops through the open gate of a screwgate karabiner. Seat the loops and lock the karabiner.

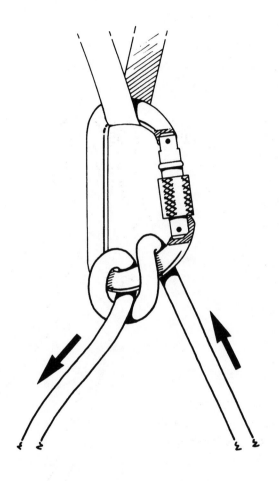

*4. Tighten the knot. The climbing rope
can now be paid out or pulled in to
provide slack or tension when required.*

ROLLING HITCH

This knot, also known as the manger's, or magnus, hitch, is basically a clove hitch with the first turn repeated. It is used in climbing as a way of securing a smaller rope to a larger one that is under strain. When the lighter rope is perpendicular to the heavier rope the knot can be easily slid along, but it will tighten as soon as lateral strain is put on the lighter rope.

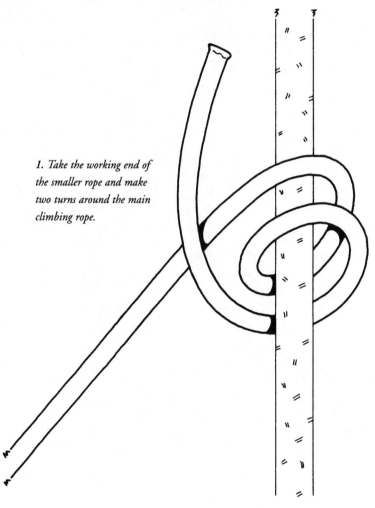

1. Take the working end of the smaller rope and make two turns around the main climbing rope.

2. Take the working end back up over the standing part, make another turn, and bring the working end out underneath the bight.

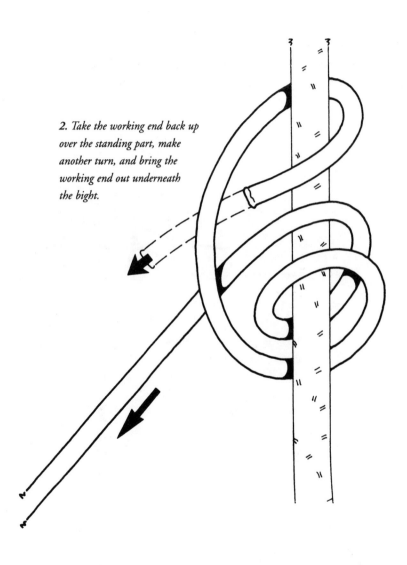

continued on page 110

Rolling Hitch

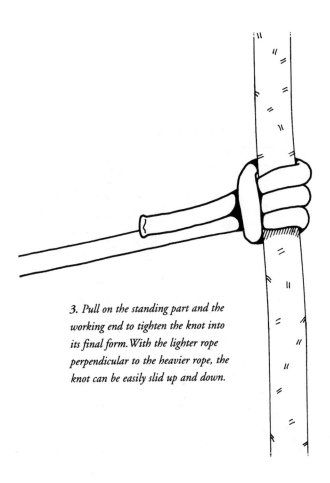

3. Pull on the standing part and the working end to tighten the knot into its final form. With the lighter rope perpendicular to the heavier rope, the knot can be easily slid up and down.

4. *As soon as lateral strain is put on the lighter rope the knot will tighten and hold firm.*

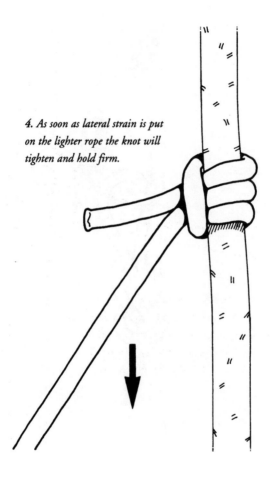

ESSENTIAL OUTDOOR KNOTS

This section describes a selection of knots that are essential for general outdoor use. Climbers, like many people who venture into the outdoors, require a basic knowledge of knots that can be used in all situations and not just the knots that are required for their particular chosen activity.

OVERHAND KNOT

Also known as the thumb knot, this knot forms the basis for many others. It is used in its own right as a stopper knot and makes a line easier to grip if tied at regular intervals along the line. A tight overhand knot can be difficult to undo if tied in very-small-diameter line or if the line becomes wet.

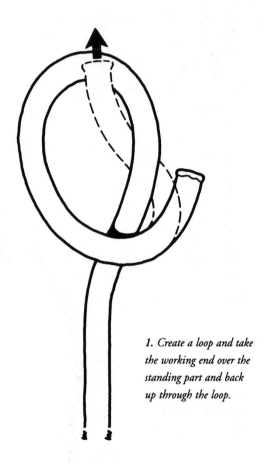

1. Create a loop and take the working end over the standing part and back up through the loop.

2. Pull on the working end and the standing part to form the final knot.

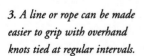

3. A line or rope can be made easier to grip with overhand knots tied at regular intervals.

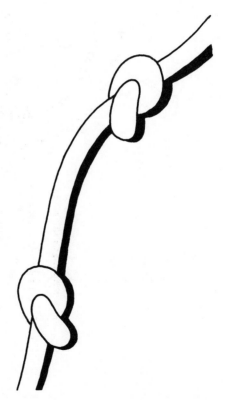

REEF KNOT

The reef knot, or square knot, is very often the only knot people know how to tie, apart from the granny knot. It gets its name from its nautical use in which two ends of a rope are tied when reefing or gathering in part of a sail.

The reef knot is not a secure knot and should not be used as one, certainly never with ropes of different diameter. It should only be used to make a temporary join in lines if identical type, weight, and diameter where it will not be put under strain. If the lines have to take strain, stopper knots should be tied in the short ends.

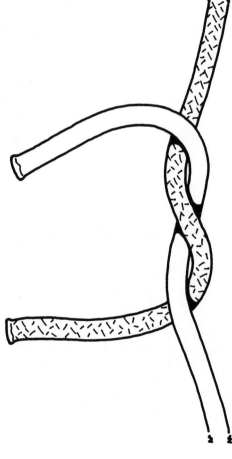

1. Bring the two working ends together and cross them left over right as shown in the illustration.

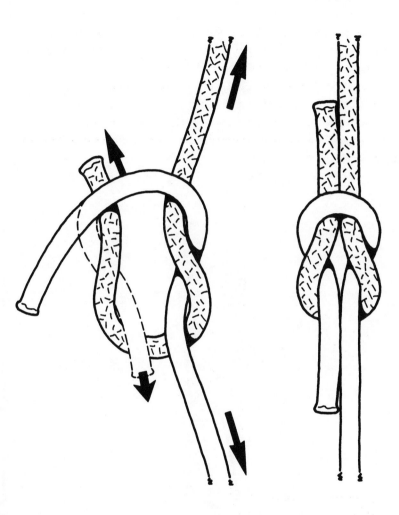

2. Now cross the two working ends right over left as shown in the illustration.

3. Tighten the knot into its final form by pulling both of the working ends and both of the standing parts.

SHEET BEND

The sheet bend is probably the most commonly used of all bends and, unlike most bends, it can safely join lines of different diameters. It is not, however, 100 percent secure and should never be used in circumstances where it will be subject to great strain. Its breaking strength also decreases in direct proportion to the difference in diameter of the lines joined.

A slipped sheet bend is formed by placing a bight between the loop of the heavier rope and the standing part of the lighter one. The slipped knot is more easily untied when the rope is under strain.

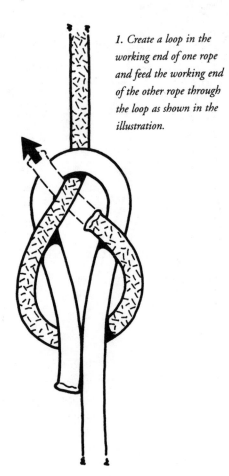

1. Create a loop in the working end of one rope and feed the working end of the other rope through the loop as shown in the illustration.

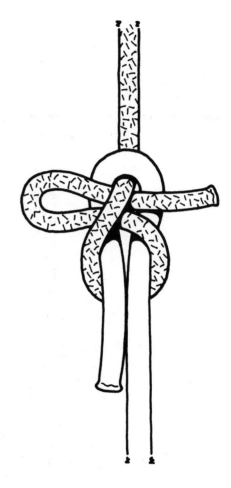

2. Pull on the standing part of both ropes to tighten the knot into its final form.

3. The slipped sheet bend is formed by placing a bight between the loop and the standing part; one sharp pull on the working end releases the knot.

FIGURE-EIGHT BEND

This simple knot (also known as the Flemish bend or knot) is tied by making a figure-eight knot in one end of a line and then following it around with the other working end. It is, despite its simplicity, one of the strongest bends and holds equally well in cord or rope.

1. Create a loose figure-eight knot in the working end of the first rope as shown in the illustration.

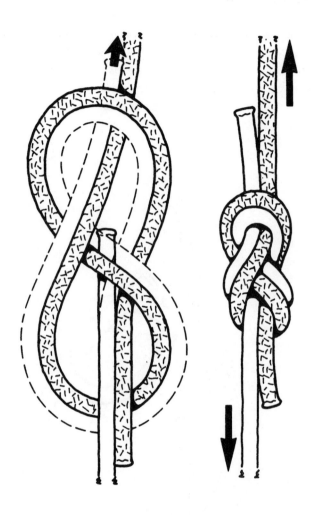

2. *Feed the working end of the second rope into the loose figure-eight formed in the first rope and follow the figure-eight pattern around as shown in the illustration.*

3. *Tighten the knot into its final form by pulling on the standing part of each rope.*

BOWLINE

The bowline is one of the best known and most widely used knots. It is tied to form a fixed loop at the end of a line or to attach a rope to an object.

The bowline's main advantages are that it does not slip, come loose, or jam. It is quick and easy to untie, even when a line is under tension, by pushing forward the bight that encircles the standing part of the line. For added security the bowline can be finished with a stopper knot.

1. Estimate the size of fixed loop required and create a small loop at that point in the standing part of the rope. Bring the working end of the rope back up and through the loop as shown in the illustration.

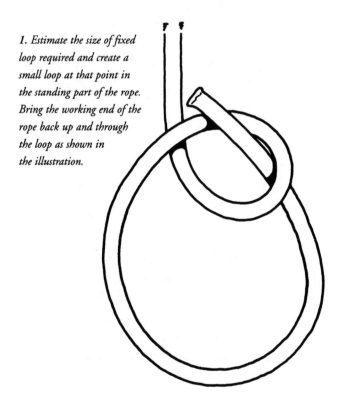

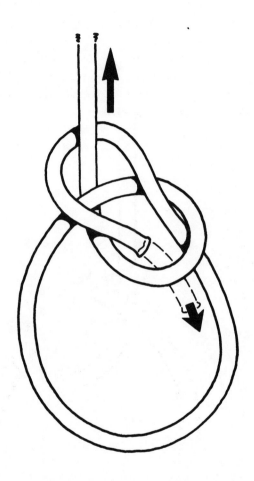

2. *Take the working end around the back of
the standing part and back down through the
loop. Then slowly start to pull on the standing
part to form the knot.*

continued on page 124

Bowline

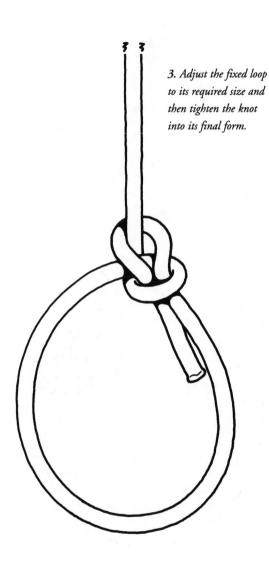

3. Adjust the fixed loop to its required size and then tighten the knot into its final form.

4. For added security the bowline can be finished with a stopper knot.

Half Hitch

The half hitch is a very widely used fastening. It is, in fact, a single hitch formed around the standing part of another hitch. It is used to complete and strengthen other knots, as in the round turn and two half hitches (see page 128), which can then be used for tying, hanging, hooking objects, etc. The slipped half hitch is a useful variation of the simple half hitch; a sharp pull on the working end releases the knot.

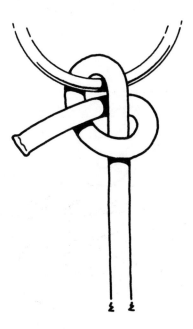

1. A single half hitch is formed by taking the working end through a ring, or similar object, back out over the standing part and through the loop. Pull on the working end and the standing part to tighten.

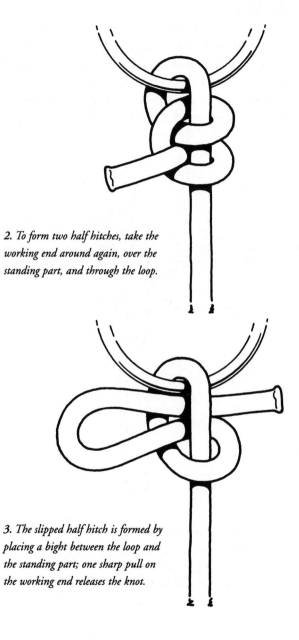

2. To form two half hitches, take the working end around again, over the standing part, and through the loop.

3. The slipped half hitch is formed by placing a bight between the loop and the standing part; one sharp pull on the working end releases the knot.

ROUND TURN AND TWO HALF HITCHES

This knot is strong, dependable, and when correctly tied, it never jams. This makes it very versatile; you can use it whenever you want to fasten a line to a ring, hook, stake, post, pole, handle, or rail. Once one end of a rope has been secured with a round turn and two half hitches, the other end can be tied with a second knot. This is especially useful for fastening down unwieldy, bulky objects.

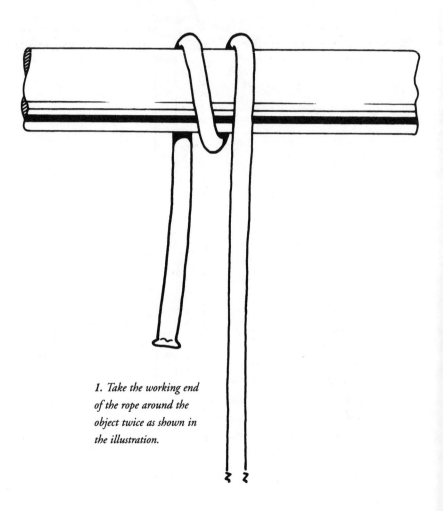

1. Take the working end of the rope around the object twice as shown in the illustration.

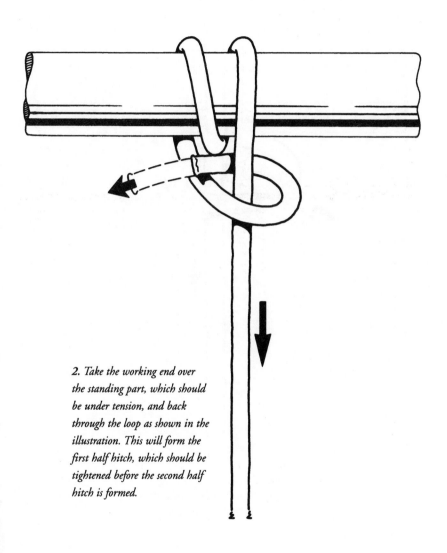

2. *Take the working end over the standing part, which should be under tension, and back through the loop as shown in the illustration. This will form the first half hitch, which should be tightened before the second half hitch is formed.*

continued on page 130

Round Turn and Two Half Hitches

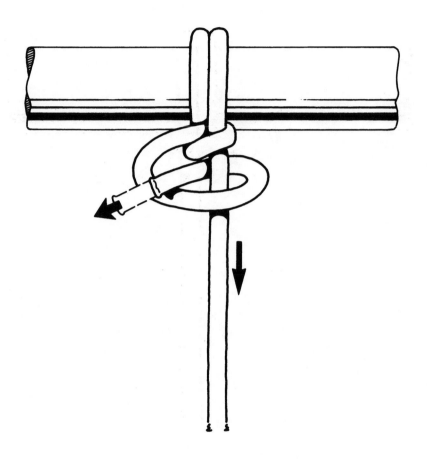

*3. Take the working end around
again to form the second half hitch.*

4. Tighten the second half hitch and then pull sharply on the standing part to form the final knot.

CONSTRICTOR KNOT

This is a popular all-purpose knot because it is firm and does not slip. It can be used as a permanent or temporary fastening. As a permanent fastening, the constrictor knot grips so firmly that if there is a need to untie it, usually the only way is to cut it free. To be sure of being able to untie it if used as a temporary fastening, the last tuck should be made with a bight to make a slip knot.

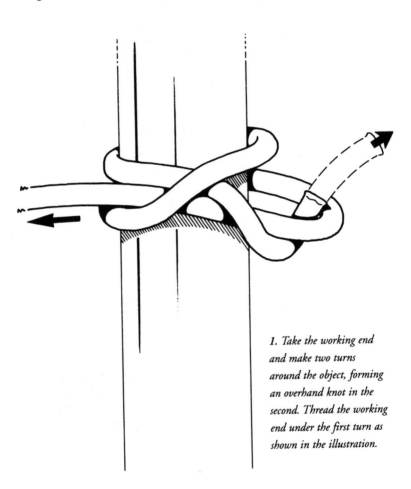

1. Take the working end and make two turns around the object, forming an overhand knot in the second. Thread the working end under the first turn as shown in the illustration.

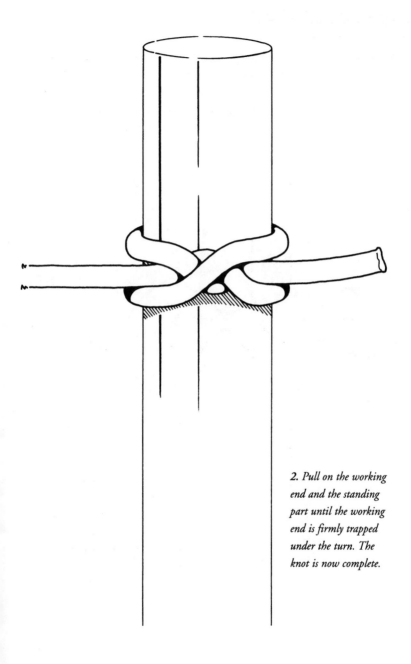

2. Pull on the working end and the standing part until the working end is firmly trapped under the turn. The knot is now complete.

FISHERMAN'S BEND

The fisherman's bend is one of the most secure and widely used hitches. It can be tied around an object or through a ring or similar device. It is a very quick knot to tie, and for additional security an additional half hitch can be added.

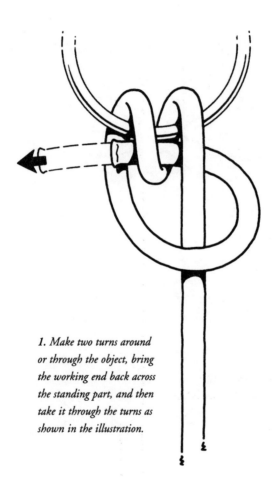

1. Make two turns around or through the object, bring the working end back across the standing part, and then take it through the turns as shown in the illustration.

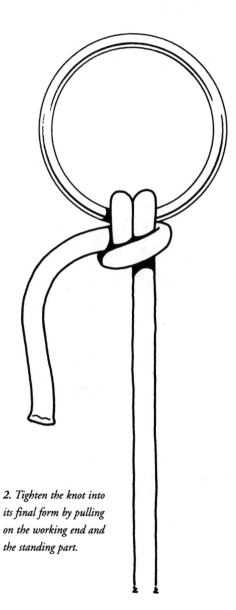

2. Tighten the knot into its final form by pulling on the working end and the standing part.

GLOSSARY

Abseiling. A method of descending a rope using friction as a control.

Belay. Anchor point on the rock face, being the position where a climber can secure himself to the rock and, by placing the ropes around his body, or to a belay device, can protect other climbers.

Bend. The action of tying two ropes together by their ends. Also the name given to the group of knots that is used to tie lines to each other or to some other object.

Bight. The slack section of the rope between the working end and the standing end. The term is particularly used when this section of the rope is formed into a loop or turned back on itself. Knots tied "in the bight" or "on the bight" do not need the ends to be used in the tying process.

Braid. To interweave several strands.

Breaking strength or **strain.** The manufacturer's estimate of the load that will cause a rope to part. This calculation is based on strength of a dry line under a steady pull; it generally takes no account of wetness, wear and tear, knots, or shock loading. Lines are weaker when worn, wet, or knotted and the manufacturer's estimate cannot, therefore, be regarded as a safe working load.

Chock. An artificial device designed to be inserted into a crack in the rock face and used as an anchor point.

Cord. The name given to several tightly twisted yarns making a line with a diameter of less than one half inch.

Cordage. Collective name for ropes and cords.

Core. The inner or central part found in ropes and in most braided lines. Formed from a bundle of parallel strands or loosely twisted yarn running the length of the rope.

Descendeur. A friction brake device used in abseiling.

Dynamic rope. A rope that stretches when under load. Main climbing ropes must be dynamic.

Eye. Loop formed at the end of a length of rope.

Free climbing. The practice of modern climbing, where no aid is used.

Hawser-laid. A type of rope construction that uses a number of twisted strands.

Heaving line. A line with a weighted knot tied at one end.

Hitch. Knot made to secure a rope to a ring, spar, etc., or to another rope.

Karabiner. A metal linking device, with a sprung gate on one side so that ropes or tapes can be easily clipped in. A **screwgate karabiner** has a threaded sleeve enabling the gate to be locked shut.

Kernmantle. Modern climbing rope made from synthetic materials and having a core of parallel fibers contained in a braided sheath.

Lay. The direction, right- or left-handed, of the twist in the strands that form a rope.

Line. Generic name for cordage with no specific purpose, although it can describe a particular use (clothesline, fishing line, etc.).

Loop. Part of a rope that is bent so that it comes together across itself.

Peg. Metal spike driven into the rock face for use as a belay.

Piton. A metal pin that can be driven into a crack in the rock face to form an anchor point.

Plain-laid rope. Three-stranded rope laid (twisted) to the right.

Plait or plat. Pronounced *plat*. To intertwine strands in a pattern.

Prusik. A technique to climb the main rope using special knots or mechanical devices (see page 96).

Route. The climb.

Sling. A loop of nylon tape or rope used to form anchors and belays.

Tying on. How a climber ties himself to the rope or to anchors.

UIAA. Union Internationale des Associations d'Alpinisme. An international body chiefly concerned with the improvement of safety standards in climbing and mountaineering.

Conversion Chart

Note: These conversion factors are not exact. They are given only
to the accuracy you're likely to need in everyday calculations.

Linear Measure

0.25 inch	= 0.6 cm
0.5 inch	= 1.25 cm
1 inch	= 2.54 cm
2 inches	= 5.08 cm
4 inches	= 10.16 cm
6 inches	= 15.25 cm
8 inches	= 20.32 cm
10 inches	= 25.40 cm
12 inches (1 foot)	= 30.48 cm
2 feet	= 0.61 m
3 feet (1 yard)	= 0.91 m
5 feet	= 1.52 m
10 feet	= 3.05 m

Measures of Weight

1 lb	= 450 g
2 lb	= 900 g
5 lb	= 2.25 kg
10 lb	= 4.5 kg
20 lb	= 9 kg
50 lb	= 23 kg
100 lb	= 46 kg

Temperature

Celsius	Fahrenheit
-17.8°	= 0°
-10°	= 14°
0°	= 32°
10°	= 50°
20°	= 68°
30°	= 86°
40°	= 104°
50°	= 122°
60°	= 140°
70°	= 158°
80°	= 176°
90°	= 194°
100°	= 212°

INDEX OF KNOTS